RALEIGH LECTURE ON HISTORY

PALMERSTON, METTERNICH, AND THE EUROPEAN SYSTEM 1830–1841[1]

By C. K. WEBSTER

Fellow of the Academy

Read 13 June 1934

HASKELL HOUSE PUBLISHERS Ltd.

Publishers of Scarce Scholarly Books

NEW YORK, N. Y. 10012

1975

HASKELL HOUSE PUBLISHERS LTD.

Publishers of Scarce Scholarly Books

280 LAFAYETTE STREET

NEW YORK. N. Y. 10012

Library of Congress Cataloging in Publication Data

Webster, Sir Charles Kingsley, 1886-1961.
  Palmerston, Metternich, and the European system,
1830-1841.

  Reprint of the 1934 ed. published by the British
Academy, London, which was issued as v. 20 of the academy's Proceedings, and as the academy's Raleigh lecture
on history, 1934.
  1. Europe--Politics and government--1815-1848--Ad-
dresses, essays, lectures. I. Title. II. Series:
British Academy, London (Founded 1901). Annual Raleigh
lecture ; 1934.
D385.W4 1975   320.9'4'0283   74-34457
ISBN 0-8383-0135-5

Printed in the United States of America

RALEIGH LECTURE ON HISTORY

PALMERSTON, METTERNICH, AND THE EUROPEAN SYSTEM 1830–1841[1]

By C. K. WEBSTER

Fellow of the Academy

Read 13 June 1934

FOR over a century the statesmen of Europe have been occupied with the attempt to create international institutions. The fundamental ideas have always been the same since they are inherent in the problem. Two great expedients have been continually in view: first that of *Conference* of the Great Powers, the creation of a central point where international affairs can be discussed verbally, instead of being transacted by exchange of notes and documents between five or six different capitals; and secondly that of *Guarantee*—of countries, frontiers, or strategic positions—the institution of a common sanction for interests which are common to all.

During the period immediately succeeding the Napoleonic wars these ideas were expressed in the European Alliance. We have now a fairly good idea of the reasons for the failure of that experiment and of the motives of the statesmen who created and destroyed it. But the period immediately succeeding, which I propose to survey to-day, though con-

[1] The Foreign Office papers in the Record Office are referred to by the name of the country and the number of the volume (e.g. *F.O. Austria*, 241). The numbers allotted to each series in the *List of Foreign Office Records* have been omitted, since none are taken from the Embassy Archives.

The papers in the *Haus, Hof- und Staatsarchiv* have been referred to in a similar manner by country and number of bundle. I am much indebted to Professor L. Bittner and Professor L. Gross for their kindness in facilitating my researches.

The papers of the first Earl Granville in the Record Office (G. and D. 29) have been referred to as *Granville Papers*.

siderably studied in recent years, is less known from this point of view. In many respects it is one of the most interesting in the century, with several new experiments, and much adaptation of old institutions to a world which is rapidly changing, as industry and finance increase in power.

The revolutions of 1830 have been to some extent neglected, because they lacked the dramatic events of those of 1848 and failed to penetrate to any large extent the great central bloc of Germany and the Hapsburg Empire. But their influence was a wide one, extending over a large part of Europe—France, Belgium, Portugal, Spain, Italy, Greece, Poland, even the Ottoman Empire itself. Europe was divided between states which adopted liberal constitutions, largely modelled on that of Britain, and those where autocracy and aristocracy still retained their hold. International relations were for a time based on community of institutions, a phenomenon which does not recur to the same degree at any other period of the century. National rivalries were momentarily subordinated to this new conception. France and Britain were for some years united by an *entente cordiale* even more intimate than that of the forties. The phrase was, indeed, first used by Palmerston himself. And Austria, Prussia, and Russia drew closely together in order to prevent the revolution spreading. Both the Eastern and Western groups were united by special treaties and each endeavoured to extend its influence into the area controlled by the other. There was a conflict of ideas between the two, in which the right of each country to choose its own rulers and institutions was fiercely debated, and the principle of *non-intervention*, which the French Minister, Molé, said he had inherited from Canning, became the catchword of European politics.

Four men dominated the period, Metternich, Palmerston, Louis Philippe, and Nicholas I, each with his own idea of a European system. All were men of exceptional energy and resource. If I dwell to-day particularly on the first two it is because I must limit my subject and they represent best the old Europe and the new. They form an engaging contrast. Metternich had nearly reached his sixtieth year and his third marriage. His great period was over. He had seen Napoleon, Castlereagh, Alexander, and Canning pass away. The Revolution which he had fought all his life had returned with a new energy and with new leaders. He was still indomitable but his attitude was that of a man almost reduced to despair. His egotism and industry remained but his energy and resource were impaired. His situation at home was weakened by the death of the Emperor Francis in 1835 and the succession of a half-wit, which enabled his opponents to undermine his power. Nevertheless he was still master of Austrian Foreign Policy, and he retained his wide outlook over Europe and his ingenious expedients to perpetuate his control over its affairs.

While Metternich did not really play a great part in the construction of the European Alliance, which was almost entirely due to Castlereagh, yet he later adopted the system as his own. He claimed that he had invented the idea of Conference in 1813, and as early as 1820 he first recorded his aspiration to make Vienna the permanent centre of the European diplomatic system.[1] He had the same desire in this period, but unfortunately hardly any one else in Europe seemed to think it a good one, except when there was great need to curry favour at Vienna. Even his Russian allies, in spite of their common hatred of the Revolution, often preferred London to Vienna. Thus Metternich was sometimes forced to suggest some more neutral place as a centre, especially Aix-la-Chapelle, which was certainly convenient geographically and perhaps recalled to Metternich tender memories of the pretty little Conference held there in 1818. But he was always convinced that European diplomacy could only be satisfactorily transacted if it revolved round himself.

Palmerston on the other hand, though half his forties were past and he had long years of office behind him, was in his

[1] Metternich, *Mémoires*, iii. 368; v. 272.

first youth as a statesman and was only to wed his Lady
Cowper at the close of this period. He had at any rate all
the energy, impetuosity, and fire of youth, qualities which
led him to commit perhaps more errors of method than any
other man who has held the office which was to be his for
sixteen out of the next twenty-one years. No less than
Metternich he wished to be the centre of European diplomacy and he threw himself into his new sphere with an
ardour and power of work which has hardly ever been
equalled, though he made successful efforts to conceal it by
cynical speech and unconventional manners. He mastered
the technical details of his business with great speed but he
introduced into it a style which was all his own. While
Grey was Premier, the Cabinet kept a firmer control over
him than under the more indolent and amiable Melbourne.
But from the first Palmerston showed so little regard for the
niceties of etiquette and diplomatic forms that his colleagues,
his subordinates, the Diplomatic Circle, and most of the
statesmen of Europe were all in a sense his bitter critics
before he had finished his first four active years. The inter-
lude, which William IV gave him by dismissing the Melbourne Ministry, was very salutary, and despite, or perhaps
because of, the efforts of foreign Powers to prevent it, he
came back in a few months stronger than ever, more popular
with the King and Commons, dominating the Cabinet and
Prime Minister, exercising an intense and rigorous control
over all his subordinates, and ready for the diplomatic
revolution that ensued.

Palmerston was fond of describing himself as a pupil of
Canning—so soon as Canning was dead. He took indeed
from him and extended that strange doctrine of *non-intervention* which had already resulted in British interference in
Portugal and Greece. But unlike his master he also showed
some enthusiasm for the idea of Conference. Grey, who
hated Canning, was sometimes for that very reason disposed
to accept the same method. Palmerston, however, like
Metternich really believed only in Conferences which he

could himself control, and it was London and not Vienna that he wanted to make the centre of the European system. At the end he had won such a triumph as rarely comes to a British statesman—at a cost which he at least did not rate very high.

The Austrian Ambassador at London and the British Ambassador at Vienna both exercised considerable influence on the policy of their Courts during this period, and both were anxious to bridge the gulf that separated Palmerston and Metternich. Prince Esterhazy was, however, often absent from his post, which he continually threatened to resign, and his subordinates, Neumann and Hummelauer, were quite incapable of dealing with the situation. Sir Frederick Lamb, later to become Lord Beauvale, also spent a good deal of time on leave, but he handled Metternich with so judicious a mixture of flattery and frankness, and kept in such close touch with the intricate machinery of the Austrian State, that he had more influence at Vienna than any other Ambassador. He was critical of his own chief, who in his turn thought his subordinate too zealous a defender of Austrian policy. But William IV, and of course his brother, the Prime Minister, no less than Metternich himself, relied on the Ambassador to restrain or divert the exuberant activities of the Secretary of State.

Palmerston inherited from his predecessors, the Wellington-Aberdeen Ministry, a position which made London the centre of the most serious of all the international complications which the revolutions of 1830 had produced. When that at Paris occurred the treaty of Quadruple Alliance, which was still valid, bound the other four Powers to meet together to decide their attitude. Wellington considered the matter with his usual thoroughness in a careful memorandum, but came to the conclusion that, though the obligation was clear, time was lacking to carry it out, and Louis Philippe was immediately recognized.[1] Metternich

---

[1] Memorandum upon the existing state of our relations with France, founded upon the Treaties of 1815-18, &c., 14 Aug. 1830, *Wellington*

at the moment was meeting Nesselrode the Russian Foreign Minister at a German Spa and reproaching him for the breach in Austrian-Russian relations which the Treaty of 1827 had caused. On the news from Paris, he proposed a reunion of the three Eastern Powers to which Britain and perhaps others should be invited. But Nesselrode, supported by Pozzo di Borgo his Ambassador at Paris, refused to agree and the *chiffon de Carlsbad*, which they drew up, was a mere statement of principle. When the Tsar's hostility to Louis Philippe became known, it was too late, and the three Powers had perforce to accept the French revolution as an accomplished fact.[1]

Meanwhile the Belgian revolution called urgently for action and the King of Holland appealed to the signatories of the Treaty of 1815. It was he, a reluctant Wellington and a determined Talleyrand who decided that the Conference should be held in London. Molé objected and suggested Paris, but it was impossible for the three Eastern Courts to transact business in a revolutionary capital. Yet even Metternich admitted that Vienna was too far away from the seat of the trouble, and thus London became the centre and Palmerston the Chairman of the Conference when he succeeded Aberdeen. No one, as Metternich bitterly lamented, quite knew what its functions were. Called by the King of Holland to consult with him, it placed him at its third meeting in the same situation as his rebellious subjects. Though the representatives of Austria, Prussia, and Russia kept together and held private meetings of their own, it was Palmerston and Talleyrand who dominated the proceedings, and the other three Courts were dragged along in their wake to recognition of a state born of revolution and the establishment by treaty of its neutral character. When the

Dispatches (*New Series*), vii. 162; Wellington to Aberdeen, 17 Aug. 1830, ibid. 178. Cf. A. C. F. Beales, *Wellington and Louis-Philippe 1830* (*History*, Mar. 1934), who, however, seems to misapprehend Wellington's attitude towards Conferences.

[1] E. Molden, *Die Orientpolitik Metternichs 1829–33*, 6–12.

King of Holland tried to assert his authority he was coerced by France and England in the name of all Europe. These decisions were in the nature of things, and it was perhaps only for form's sake that Metternich, when it was too late, chided his representatives for going too far. But he was bitterly conscious of his impotence and anxious to withdraw other European affairs from so dangerous a neighbourhood.

In 1831, therefore, when negotiations for a reduction in armaments began in Europe, though he responded to the French offer to send Plenipotentiaries to meet those of the other Powers 'in any town which might be fixed upon', he suggested immediately Aix-la-Chapelle as a convenient centre for the discussions.[1] To his horror, however, the Tsar showed a strange predilection for London and appeared to be ready to discuss this or any other major question there. Fortunately Prince Lieven, the Russian Ambassador, more experienced of Palmerston, was not of the same opinion, and Metternich hastened to show that the place was impossible, if for no other reason, because England herself was rapidly being engulfed by the Revolution. Palmerston would have been glad to have the four Powers discuss the matter informally at London, but, partly by reason of these jealousies, no centre was ever fixed upon and the disarmament negotiations dwindled into generalities and were never brought to fruition.[2] That Metternich had intended this negotiation to develop into a Conference on European questions at Vienna we know from Russian sources. Almost at the same time he had proposed a special meeting of Plenipotentiaries of the three Eastern Courts. But the Tsar

---

[1] Cowley to Palmerston, 7 May 1831, *F. O. Austria*, 228; Granville to Palmerston, 23 May 1831, *F.O. France*, 429.

[2] Wessenberg to Metternich, 12 June 1831, *W. St. A. England*, 252; Metternich to Esterhazy, 14 June 1831, *W. St. A. England*, 254; Metternich, *Mémoires*, v. 162, 207. Metternich rejected the idea of limitation as a chimaera. It was to be simply a question of reducing armed forces to a peace footing.

quite realized the real object, for he noted on his Ambassador's report 'Voilà le grand désir de. Metternich, celui d'être *à la tête* des affaires, clair et nettement prononcé'.[1]

In 1832 Metternich's hostility to the Belgian Conference increased. He scolded his representative on it for his servility to Palmerston and Talleyrand. The ratifications of the Treaty constituting Belgium were only obtained from the three Eastern Powers with the greatest difficulty, and when Metternich's arrived, heralded by much parade, it was found to be meaningless, since it depended on Russia's, which in turn depended on the King of Holland. 'Metternich has made April Fools of us' wrote Palmerston in disgust . . . 'It is only a piece of parchment which might as well be at Vienna as in London, on the back of its own sheep as in the hands of Neumann.'[2]

The visit of Orlov, the Tsar's confidant, at last resolved this position, but when further measures of coercion against Holland were at last put into force the Conference virtually broke up. Metternich complained that it was too far off for him to control his representatives adequately. He suggested therefore that the Conference should be renewed in another place. The Hague would be best, he wrote, but if England and France thought that impossible, then Aix-la-Chapelle midway between that place and Brussels. Prussian support was obtained and Metternich hoped that of Russia also; but unfortunately Bülow, the Prussian Minister at London, anticipated his colleagues with Palmerston, who immediately announced that he would have nothing to do with the proposal. 'To do so', he told Lord Granville his Ambassador at Paris, 'would be to throw a slur upon the members of the Conference of London.' He defended its procedure in a warm altercation with Neumann at a dinner party: 'We are on an equal footing', he said, 'and we are so according to the principles of the Grand Alliance created at

[1] F. Martens, *Recueil des Traités et Conventions conclus par la Russie*, **iv**, part i. 425.

[2] Palmerston to Granville, 6 Apr. 1832, *Granville Papers*, Box 14.

Chaumont and confirmed at the Congresses of Vienna, Aix-la-Chapelle, and Verona. If you have thought fit to separate yourself from it, it is not our fault.' The Conference, therefore, was not resumed and the five Powers remained separated into two and three.[1]

Yet there was urgent need for Europe to be united, for the defeat of the Sultan by the troops of his vassal, Mehemet Ali, the ruler of Egypt, had raised the Eastern Question in an acute form. Here Austrian interests were the same as those of Britain and France and divided from those of Russia. But Metternich had perforce to support the Tsar, though he was for a time far more interested in the conservation of the Ottoman Empire than Palmerston himself. 'The fact is,' Palmerston had written in an intimate letter in 1831, 'Turkey is falling rapidly to pieces,'[2] and he seemed to view the process with some complacency. Nor was he at first so alarmed as Metternich at the proceedings of Mehemet Ali, who he thought might possibly make a good substitute for the Sultan. What he feared was the advance of Russia, whose actions at Constantinople he regarded with the greatest suspicion. But this was an attitude with which Metternich did not dare to agree. He tried to obtain Palmerston's support on other grounds but only secured the suggestion of a Guarantee of the integrity of the Turkish dominions, while Talleyrand proposed a self-denying declaration by all the Great Powers.[3]

It was at this point that Metternich first put forward the idea that Vienna should be made the centre of a common negotiation on the Eastern Question. Since Palmerston's responses had not been satisfactory, it was to Paris and not

[1] Metternich to Neumann, 25 December 1832, *W. St. A. England*, 261; Lamb to Palmerston, 26 December 1832, *F.O. Austria*, 236; Granville to Palmerston, 31 Dec. 1832, *F.O. France*, 450; Palmerston to Granville, 3 Jan. 1833, *F.O. France*, 461; Neumann to Metternich, 8 Jan. 1833, *W. St. A. England*, 262; E. B. Chancellor, *Diary of Philipp von Neumann*, i. 281.

[2] Palmerston to Granville, 3 June 1831, *Granville Papers*, Box 14.

[3] Granville to de Broglie, 26 Apr. 1833, *Granville Papers*, Box 16.

to London that the proposal was first sent. It was associated with the specific of guarantee, but the whole scheme was adumbrated, in that tentative manner of which Metternich was a master, in conversations with Sainte-Aulaire, the French Ambassador at Vienna, and in instructions to Apponyi, the Austrian Ambassador at Paris. Metternich was clearly not sure of his ground and was feeling his way, but of his intense desire to make Vienna the central point of the negotiation there can be no doubt. He expressed it on every possible occasion to the French Ambassador.[1]

Palmerston was not at first consulted directly but of course he soon heard of the scheme from his subordinates. He also thought the Eastern Question needed discussion at a centre but he wished it to be at London and not at Vienna. He had already expressed to Neumann his regret that the Conference on Belgium had been suspended, since it might have proved convenient for this purpose. Talleyrand had already made the same suggestion with the object of isolating Russia. But Talleyrand treated Metternich's new proposal very differently to Palmerston. The two agreed that some self-denying agreement by the Powers should be one of its principal objects. But while Talleyrand, who was already jealous of Palmerston's intimate relations with his chief the Duc de Broglie, was prepared to accept Vienna as the centre of discussion, Palmerston absolutely refused. He suggested instead that the Convention should be signed at Constantinople itself, and when Neumann pointed out the difficulties in the way, insinuated that he might sign it himself, plainly indicating, as Metternich noted on the margin of the despatch, that London was to be made the centre of discussion.[2] He naturally got no encouragement from Neumann and a week later announced that he had

---

[1] Lamb to Palmerston, 13 April 1833, *F.O. Austria*, 241; Granville to Palmerston, 27 May 1833, *F.O. France*, 465; Stern, *Geschichte Europas*, iv. 490; Comte de Sainte-Aulaire, *Souvenirs*, 229.

[2] Neumann to Metternich, 26 Mar., 1, 12, 23, 26 Apr., 10 May 1833, *W. St. A. England*, 263, 264.

abandoned the plan. The Cabinet had refused it, he said, because it would lead to a Conference and the manner in which the three Eastern Powers had behaved in the Belgian question had made the idea of a five-power Conference most unpalatable. The whole transaction, reported Neumann, showed that, even if Palmerston were relieved of the Belgian difficulty, he would at once seek for other questions with which to embarrass Austria. Metternich at once revealed this criticism to Lamb who promptly reported it to London. Palmerston was furious at the charge and heaped abuse on Neumann, whom he never afterwards quite forgave.[1]

Yet Palmerston had indicated on more than one occasion that he would have accepted the Conference, if London and not Vienna had been made the place of negotiation. He confessed as much in a private letter to Lamb, which the latter showed to Metternich. 'The state of things in the East', he wrote, 'is far from satisfactory and I agree entirely with you that the only way to have arranged them promptly and well would have been for the four Powers to have concerted together the measures to be taken last October. But whose fault was it? First and foremost it was the fault of Russia who broke up the [Belgian] Conference, which, if it had gone on, would by keeping up confidential communications between the five Powers have afforded facilities for an understanding upon affairs of the East.'[2] Metternich was moved to indignation by this confession.

Ce plan [he protested in a private letter] n'était autre que celui de rendre la conférence de Londres pour ainsi dire permanente; de l'élever peu à peu à la hauteur d'une institution politique en lui attribuant la valeur et l'influence d'un aréopage, dans lequel les représentans des trois Puissances continentales eûssent été réduits

[1] Neumann to Metternich, 21 May 1833, W. St. A. England, 264; Lamb to Palmerston, 3 June 1833, F.O. Austria, 242; Palmerston to Lamb, 11 June 1833 (Private), W. St. A. England Varia, 29; Palmerston to Lamb, 18 June 1833, F.O. Austria, 239; E. B. Chancellor, Diary of Philipp von Neumann, i. 286, 287.

[2] Extract from a private letter from Palmerston to Lamb, 17 May 1833, W. St. A. England Varia, 29.

au rôle de complices de la politique réformatrice des deux cours maritimes.[1]

It was too bad of Palmerston to have exactly the same plan of making a European centre as Metternich himself!

Throughout this period of stress Metternich had continued to defend against every insinuation of Palmerston the good faith of the Tsar. This he did in spite of the Tsar's strange reluctance to accept Metternich's guidance on all the affairs of Europe especially on those of the East. But now came the first of the blows which Russia dealt to his pride. It showed how precarious was the intimacy of which he boasted. When the news first came from French sources of the Treaty of Unkiar Skelessi between Russia and Turkey Metternich refused to believe it. There can be no doubt of his humiliation when he learnt that it was true. He for long refused to discuss it and instead heaped reproaches on Britain and France for refusing the Conference at Vienna. It was not until December after his return from München-grätz that the painful subject could be openly approached. Then Metternich assured Lamb that he had told the Tsar: 'I took a guarantee for your conduct which has been falsified. . . . Should I ever feel myself called upon hereafter to answer for the conduct of your Government what can I expect from France and England but that they should reply: "Dupe once, you may be deceived again"?'

'This frank and humiliating avowal', was the Ambassador's comment, 'must have cost him much, but it was the best line he could take, nor shall I again recur to the subject.'[2]

The so-called Conference at Münchengrätz in the late summer of 1833 between the three Eastern Powers was held partly as a sop to Metternich's feelings. He had long desired such a meeting. There the Tsar overwhelmed him with flattery and obtained his unqualified

[1] Metternich to Neumann, 9 June 1833, *W. St. A. England*, 267.

[2] Lamb to Palmerston, 5 July, 1 Oct., 26 Dec. 1833, *F.O. Austria*, 242, 243.

support for Russia's Eastern policy. The three Eastern Courts also sent a warning to France on the right of intervention to which de Broglie replied with spirit and discretion.

All this made Palmerston even more suspicious than before not only of Russia but also of Austria. For long he suspected that a secret treaty for the partition of the Ottoman Empire had been made at Münchengrätz, and would not listen to Lamb's attempts to explain Metternich's attitude. He did indeed allow Esterhazy on his arrival to bring about an apparent reconciliation between himself and Lieven with whom he had hardly been on speaking terms, but he told the latter that peace and war were in the Emperor's hands.[1]

He continued to believe and assert that Austria had become the slave of Russia owing to her fear of revolution. Metternich now found, however, a willing listener in Talleyrand, who like himself had been pushed on one side. They began a secret correspondence which was shared by the Austrian Ambassadors at London and Paris. But Metternich was still anxious to make himself the centre of negotiations on the Eastern Question and put forward several feelers to France and England in 1834. He desired them to use Austria as the intermediary with Russia over the Treaty of Unkiar Skelessi rather than the direct method of protest which they preferred. He wished a new instrument to be negotiated at Vienna in which the treaty should be turned into one in which all the Powers should share. Lamb made the most of these advances, but Palmerston was obdurate, and Metternich lamented that, though Austrian and British interests were identical, he could not enter into communication with London.[2] There was not the slightest evidence, however, that Russia would concur in his plans.

---

[1] Lieven to Nesselrode, 27 Dec. 1833, *W. St. A. England*, 268.

[2] Esterhazy to Metternich, 10 Jan. 1834, *W. St. A. England*, 268; Lamb to Palmerston, 18 Feb., 15 Mar., 19 July, 2 Nov. (Nos. 1, 2, 3 Private and Confidential), 1834, *F.O. Austria*, 247, 248.

On the contrary the Tsar, while ready to go to any length with Metternich against revolution in the West, had not the slightest intention of accepting his guidance in the East.

L'Autriche [reported Nesselrode ironically to his master at the end of 1834] s'est entièrement convaincue du désintéressement de la politique russe à l'égard de la Turquie et a même consenti, quoique non sans regret, à assumer un rôle secondaire dans la question d'Orient.[1]

But in 1834 the main focus of events had shifted, and Palmerston had obtained in the Spanish Peninsula a triumph that compensated him for the check in the East. In that quarter he had always meant to keep out all interference by the Eastern Powers. Thus he agreed easily enough to a French expedition to coerce the Portuguese usurper, and when the three Powers attempted to influence events he told Lieven that he saw in their action 'le doigt de la Sainte Alliance'.[2]

On the death of Ferdinand of Spain he organized his defence of the little Queens without even a reference to the Eastern Courts. It is significant, however, and a sign of his rashness and immaturity that he at first desired to leave France out also or at least to reduce her to a secondary role. The mistake was all the more patent since France had consistently paid deference to the superiority of British interests in Portugal. Palmerston acquiesced, however, in Talleyrand's protests and the Quadruple Treaty of April 1834 was regarded throughout Europe as a counterblow to the alliance of the three Eastern Powers. It took constitutions as well as Queens under its aegis and the doctrine of nonintervention, which had been so loudly proclaimed, was certainly given a most Canningite interpretation. But for the moment it served its purpose, and Palmerston rejoiced in a coup, which he had carried through against the wishes of the majority of his own Cabinet including some of his Canningite friends.

[1] F. Martens, *Recueil*, iv, part i. 467.
[2] Neumann to Metternich, 29 June 1832, *W. St. A. England*, 258.

In spite of this success, when Palmerston's first period of office closed, Britain was in a sufficiently dangerous condition. The conflict with Russia had been embittered by the departure of the Lievens, Prussia and Austria were aloof and hostile, Talleyrand had left 'profondément dégoûté', full of rancour and already intriguing against the Entente which he had done so much to establish.[1] Metternich had already rejoiced at the resignation of Grey and ordered his representative to transact business with the new Prime Minister, Melbourne, and to avoid intercourse with Palmerston as much as possible.[2] The appearance of Don Carlos in the north of Spain was a portent of disaster and, though a new Convention was negotiated with France, the Eastern Powers had now a champion in the West. Perhaps it was with something like relief that Palmerston in a hasty postscript sent the news to Vienna of the dismissal of the Melbourne Ministry. 'We are out . . .', he wrote, 'lose no time in telling Metternich. I am sure that he will never have been more happy than in reading the news.' Metternich returned a verbose and sententious answer to the effect that not joy but hope was the emotion which moved him.[3]

Honours in the first round between the two statesmen were in fact evenly divided. They had thwarted one another in East and West though often admitting that their interests were nearly the same. Palmerston had Belgium and the Quadruple Alliance to his credit. Metternich had kept his grip on Italy and Germany at the cost of some concessions to Prussia. The allies of both were unreliable. In the Eastern Question Russia had profited by their rivalry to establish her influence at Constantinople. Neither had succeeded in creating round himself that centre of European diplomacy to which each had aspired.

[1] Hummelauer to Metternich, 7 Aug. 1834, *W. St. A. England*, 270.

[2] Metternich to Hummelauer, 11 Sept. 1834, *W. St. A. England*, 272.

[3] Metternich to Hummelauer, 29 Nov. 1834, Metternich, *Mémoires*, v. 642.

Both the three Eastern Courts and Louis Philippe hastened to show their sense of relief when the Whigs fell. Palmerston lost his seat in Hampshire to Metternich's great delight and his position in public life seemed to have deteriorated. The Austrian Ambassador returned to his post. France and Russia hastened to appoint eminent successors to Talleyrand and Lieven. The Prussian Minister showed himself once more at the King's levee. 'Le Roi et ses ministres en ont été fort flattés' reported Esterhazy.[1] But in spite of these attentions the situation of the Tory Ministry was obviously a precarious one. It was too weak to alter Palmerston's policy, showed a lamentable dislike of Don Carlos, and would not even venture to recall Lord Ponsonby from Constantinople. The great thing therefore was to prevent Palmerston coming back with the Whigs to the Foreign Office. Lamb, who had returned home, would, it was hoped, use his influence with Melbourne to this end. The Ambassador did indeed visit the King at Brighton and give him much salutary advice. The Ministers of the three Eastern Powers went farther. For they approached Lansdowne and Grey, who they expected to return as Prime Minister, to urge that the Foreign Office should be given to any one rather than Palmerston. But these magnates treated them with the greatest haughtiness and disdain. Such clumsy efforts, as Metternich noted on Esterhazy's mournful dispatch, were calculated to defeat their own ends. Though 'Bear' Ellice was as usual intriguing against Palmerston, it became only too clear that he was coming back and that they must make the best of him. 'Do not let Metternich think', wrote Lamb in a private note to Esterhazy, 'that everything will go ill if we have Palmerston back again. My mission here was to improve him not to change him.'[2]

So Palmerston came back to a position which was full of complications. The tide of feeling against Russia was run-

---

[1] Esterhazy to Metternich, 21 Feb. 1835, *W. St. A. England*, 273.

[2] Esterhazy to Metternich, 27 Mar. 1835; Lamb to Esterhazy, 27 Mar. 1835, *W. St. A. England*, 273.

ning high and was strongly felt by the King. Relations with France on the other hand were obviously much worse, though Palmerston did not know that Louis Philippe had already told the Austrian Ambassador that his return to favour would be so great a misfortune that the King could hardly believe it possible.[1]

The great question now was Spain, where Palmerston's work was gravely threatened by the Carlist revolt. Though the Eastern Powers dared not recognize Don Carlos, they supplied him with funds and supplies. Behind both parties to the cruel and devastating civil war were groups of European financiers, stock-exchange speculators, and mushroom armament firms. But there was also a conflict of principle in this sordid setting, and in June 1835 Palmerston horrified Metternich by a speech which identified the interests of Britain with the constitutional cause. He haughtily refused all explanation and told the Prussian Minister, who had ventured to protest, that he believed the three Eastern Courts had a secret treaty to put down Constitutionalism in Europe. Metternich washed his hands of him, and ordered Esterhazy to use only Melbourne for diplomatic business, a task which the Ambassador found rather difficult, except when Lamb was there to influence his brother.[2] Metternich therefore turned towards France, and the intimate confidences between Louis Philippe and Austria increased. The French King showed great anxiety to heal the breach between East and West. He even put forward the idea that a Conference should be held, not for any particular purpose, but to demonstrate the common interests of the Five Powers and that they desired to live at peace without interfering in each other's internal affairs. It was true that he suggested London as the best place for this meeting, but it was clear to both Esterhazy and Apponyi that Anglo-French relations

[1] Apponyi to Metternich, 7 Apr. 1835, *W. St. A. Frankreich*, 421.

[2] Esterhazy to Metternich, 25 June, 10, 31 July, 7, 16 Aug. 1835, *W. St. A. England*, 275; Metternich to Esterhazy, 16 July 1835, *W. St. A. England*, 280.

had changed and the King's geographical notions might be improved. The process was delayed by a speech of the Tsar at Warsaw to the unfortunate Poles, which roused France to fury, and the necessity of British help in settling a dangerous dispute between France and the United States. But Louis was obviously going in the right direction.[1]

It was at this period, December 1835, that Palmerston suggested to his friend de Broglie a Treaty of Guarantee of the Ottoman Empire. The French Government was persuaded to accept the scheme and proposed that it should be in the first instance offered to the Sultan by France and England, the other Powers being subsequently invited to join. De Broglie even offered to include in it a guarantee against attack by Mehemet Ali, so as to outbid the Treaty of Unkiar Skelessi. The exact form was for some time a matter of debate between the two Governments carried on exclusively in private letters. But de Broglie and Palmerston were in substantial agreement that England and France must first act together alone, and submit a *fait accompli* to Metternich, who, though he was not likely to accept it, would be secretly pleased to have such a weapon against Russia ready to his hand.[2]

At this point, however, Louis Philippe intervened and refused his assent unless the Treaty were immediately opened for signature to all the Powers, including Russia, and extended to a territorial guarantee of the whole of Europe. De Broglie protested that no one would sign such a treaty, but at the King's insistence he made the proposal to Palmerston. No notice was taken of it and so far as Britain was concerned the idea seems to have been dropped.[3] Shortly afterwards

[1] Apponyi to Metternich, 24 Oct. 1835, *W. St. A. Frankreich*, 422; Esterhazy to Metternich, 3 Sept. 1835 (Particulière), *W. St. A. England*, 276. For the effect of the American dispute on the situation see my article 'British Mediation between France and the United States in 1834–6', in *English Historical Review*, January 1927.

[2] Granville to Palmerston, 11, 18, 28 Dec. 1835, *Granville Papers*, Box 14.

[3] Apponyi to Metternich, 24 Jan. 1836, *W. St. A. Frankreich*, 425.

the Doctrinaires lost office and de Broglie was replaced at the Foreign Office by Thiers, a nominee of Talleyrand and Princess Lieven, and not therefore expected to be a friend of Britain. The *entente cordiale* was obviously wearing thin.

The year 1836 brought indeed a great change in Anglo-French relations, and Louis Philippe turned definitely towards Austria and away from Britain, though some of his Ministers refused to follow him. The change was partly due to dynastic reasons, for it was in this year that Louis made his famous attempt to marry his son to an Austrian Princess. But it was also due to his dread of being forced into a more active policy in Spain by Palmerston's impetuous demands, which Thiers supported though not otherwise a friend of British policy. Metternich, who had access through a spy to the innermost secrets of the French Court and Cabinet, played Louis Philippe in his most skilful manner. Events in Spain, he hoped, would overthrow Palmerston, and the three Eastern Courts prepared to recognize their champion Don Carlos as soon as he reached Madrid. At the same time Metternich hoped to draw France into the orbit of Austrian policy and through her European affairs to Vienna. Palmerston, he more than once triumphantly announced, was isolated and powerless.[1]

Louis Philippe was indeed feverishly anxious to ingratiate himself. He began by revealing to Apponyi under the pledge of deepest secrecy the discussions as to the guarantee of the integrity of the Ottoman Empire which had taken place at the end of 1835 between France and England, and of his own counter proposals of a general guarantee.

Dans l'esprit de ce traité [he explained] aucun changement, aucune aliénation de territoire n'auroit pu dorénavant avoir lieu sans le concours de toutes les Puissances — et j'aurais vu se réaliser

---

[1] Metternich to Hummelauer, 9 May 1836. 'La punition véritable de la ligne politique sur laquelle Lord Palmerston s'est engagé doit être celle de faire peser sur l'Angleterre un isolement qu'aucune Puissance — si j'en excepte l'Empire de la Chine — ne peut supporter à la longue', *W. St. A. England*, 280.

enfin cette idée que je poursuis continuellement d'une entente
entre les cinqu Puissances pour la solution de toutes les grandes
questions politiques.

Unfortunately, he confessed, no reply had come from
England, thus showing *her* object to be something quite
different. A little later he informed Apponyi that Prussia
was favourable to the idea of a Conference of the Five
Powers, but had strangely enough suggested that it should
be established at London, where the Belgian Conference
had nearly accomplished that desirable result. Louis
Philippe himself had not very long ago made the same proposal but he now had a completely different view.

C'est chez vous à Vienne [he told Apponyi] que selon moi cette
entente devroit s'établir, et puis je ne veux pas *pour une affaire seule
ou de préférence*, mais *pour toutes les questions dans un intérêt général et
Européen*. Ah! si la Russie vouloit, nous établirions bientôt cette
entente si désirable entre les cinqu Puissances *pour garantir le statu
quo de la délimitation territoriale en Europe*.

A little later he returned to the attack on the same theme
and claimed that Lord William Russell had informed him
on his way through Paris to Berlin that Melbourne was
most favourable to the idea, though Palmerston was against
it. It transpired, however, that Melbourne was not prepared to include Russia, and Talleyrand insisted that
England was really aiming at an offensive and defensive
alliance with France. Metternich accepted this conclusion
and pointed out that the time was not ripe for Louis' great
scheme. Louis Philippe reluctantly gave way and the pro-
ject was put on one side once more.[1]

Still more significant was Louis Philippe's next move.
His son was now at the Court of Vienna and he was loading
Metternich with flattery. Meanwhile the difficulties of the
Spanish question were increasing and the King was appeal-
ing to Metternich for sympathy at the trying position in
which Palmerston and Thiers were placing him. The latter

[1] Apponyi to Metternich, 24 Jan., 4, 21 Feb., 3, 24 Mar., 12 May
1836, *W. St. A. Frankreich* 425, 426.

had indeed made his own approach to Austria by a suggestion that the son of Don Carlos should marry the young Queen—an offer not sufficiently legitimist to win Metternich's consent. Now at the orders of his King he proposed to Britain that the Spanish question should be submitted to a Conference of the *five* Powers. Palmerston naturally rejected this scheme with great indignation as equivalent to allowing the three Eastern Courts to interfere in Spanish affairs against the spirit of the Quadruple Alliance. It was immediately communicated by Louis Philippe to Metternich and doubtless it was for that purpose that it had been made.[1]

Thus on neither of the two questions, that of the Ottoman Empire and that of the Peninsula, was any contact made between the five Powers, and Europe remained divided into East and West. But France in spite of the check she received by the failure of Louis' flattery to win an Austrian Princess was now at any rate no longer influenced by England; and when Thiers was too eager in the cause of the Spanish Queen, his King got rid of him.

In these circumstances Palmerston was more ready than before to adopt the advice which Lamb was constantly urging that an understanding could be arrived at with Austria. The British Ambassador had with great tact and skill extracted from Metternich a promise of Austrian support for Britain if Russia attacked the Ottoman dominions either in Europe or Asia. It was true that Metternich declared such a contingency impossible, and urged Britain to use a more friendly tone towards Russia, but Lamb thought that, if it was desirable, he could obtain from him a formal guarantee of the Ottoman Empire. Palmerston's embarrassments in the West made him contemplate the acceptance of Metternich's advice. There was a revolution in Spain and the conduct of Louis Philippe grew continually more equivocal. Both Palmerston and Melbourne admitted that Russia was perhaps less dangerous than they had

[1] Apponyi to Metternich, 13 June 1836, *W. St. A. Frankreich*, 426.

supposed. Palmerston even condescended to explain his Spanish policy to Esterhazy. Metternich covered the dispatch with sarcastic comments but nevertheless the two had come closer together and the reply was not unfriendly. At the end of December Palmerston told Esterhazy that paradoxical as it might seem he believed Austria and Britain to be the only two really conservative Powers, that is, Powers which really desired to keep the *status quo* in Europe. It was clear that national interests, as Durham had long ago urged, were resuming their control over policy.[1]

Next year the Spanish question eased somewhat; but the rivalry between England and Russia flared up again in the matter of the 'Vixen'. Metternich importantly assumed the office of mediator and promised to support the British case at Petersburg. The Tsar rebuffed him and he immediately withdrew, much to Lamb's disgust. But it was France and Mehemet that Palmerston now distrusted even more than Russia and he settled the dispute by a convenient fiction. There were signs also that Austria was becoming less subservient to Russia, and Lamb was able to report a distinct change of attitude. Esterhazy was trying to persuade Metternich that Palmerston had undergone a similar process and, if Metternich refused to agree, his tone became less bitter.[2] Both Palmerston and Metternich therefore were by 1838, in spite of some alarms, ready for a *rapprochement* on the Eastern Question. Each began that year preparations to solve it, but each planned to make himself the centre of the necessary discussions.

Palmerston's opportunity came with the reopening of the Belgian question. The King of Holland at last consented to accept the decisions of 1831 and consequently the discussions were resumed at London. A conference centre was

---

[1] Lamb to Palmerston, 5 Aug. 1836, *F.O. Austria*, 257; Esterhazy to Metternich, 2 Nov., 30 Dec. 1836, *W. St. A. England*, 279.

[2] Lamb to Palmerston, 3, 25 Feb., 5 Mar., 21 April, 22 Sept. 1837, *F.O. Austria*, 264, 265; Metternich to Hummelauer, 2 Nov. 1837, *W. St. A. England*, 283.

thus established there, and, as in 1832, Palmerston sought to use it as an instrument to settle the Eastern Question. His suspicions of France grew this year, for Molé, who was now back in power, was known to wish for an accommodation with Russia, and the interests of the two countries might easily be reconciled if Nicholas could overcome his personal hostility to Louis Philippe.

News now came that Mehemet Ali was about to declare himself independent. Palmerston thought action necessary to make him realize that such a defiance of the Sultan would not be tolerated. At first a joint declaration by England and France seemed the safest and quickest method. But this was soon abandoned for a negotiation at London for a common declaration of all the five Powers. By this means Palmerston hoped to deal at the same time with both the Egyptian and the Russian threat to the Porte, for the declaration, besides stopping Mehemet, would substitute for the treaty of Unkiar Skelessi an instrument which would place the Sultan under the protection of all the Great Powers.[1]

Sebastiani, the French Ambassador, always a good friend to Britain, entered warmly into this plan. The French Government shuffled and hesitated but eventually seemed to acquiesce. Metternich welcomed the idea of a joint declaration, which he claimed had been his own policy for some time, but did not commit himself as to the place of negotiation. Unfortunately just at this moment a new and violent dispute with Russia over Persia complicated matters. Public opinion in Britain was again stirred up against her and strong language was again used. On the question of Mehemet, however, Russia was responsive. Palmerston therefore tried to go on with his scheme and he summoned the representatives of the four Powers to meet him at the Foreign Office. No object was specified in the invitation and it might very well have been for some purpose connected with the Belgian problem. But there had been previous

[1] Palmerston to Granville, 5, 8 June, 6 July 1838, H. L. Bulwer, *Life of Palmerston*, ii. 266–72.

indications that Palmerston wanted to bring the Eastern Question to the London Conference and the representatives of the three Powers consulted together beforehand as to their attitude. They decided to go, but to be non-committal, and Esterhazy paid a visit to Palmerston before the meeting to warn him that he should make it clear that the occasion was only for the purpose of explaining the views of the British Government. Palmerston admitted the irregularity of the procedure, but refused to change it. At the meeting he dwelt on the necessity of establishing a common attitude towards Mehemet Ali amongst the five Powers and suggested that the Ambassadors should ask their Courts for instructions, so that it could be negotiated in London. Sebastiani declared that he had them already, Pozzo di Borgo took refuge in complete silence, Esterhazy and Bülow took the matter *ad referendum*.[1] This was not very encouraging; but Palmerston followed with a note to Pozzo 'proposing that the representatives of the five Powers in London should concert together as to the measures which might become necessary if Mehemet Ali should persist in declaring himself independent of the Porte'. Pozzo was vastly alarmed at the idea of the whole question being submitted to a conference in London, and Nesselrode's answer was that it was not necessary since the action of the five Powers at Constantinople would be sufficient. In reply Palmerston admitted that this might be the case, but added that it was also necessary to concert together on the method of assisting the Sultan, if hostilities broke out. Britain would not allow Russia to act alone another time, he insisted, since there would be a natural fear that further concessions might be exacted from the Porte as the price of her help: 'That therefore the only way in which Turkey could be assisted without risking a disturbance of the peace of Europe would be by the establishment of that concert between the five

---

[1] Metternich to Esterhazy, 25 June 1838 (Particulière), *W. St. A. England*, 283; Esterhazy to Metternich, 18 Aug. 1838, *W. St. A. England*, 285.

Powers which Her Majesty's Government have proposed.'[1] There can be no doubt that this declaration had a great effect on Russian policy when the crisis came in 1839.

At the moment, however, there was great tension between Russia and England and nothing further could be done. Metternich was more amenable, but the result was the same. When Lamb carefully pointed out that it was merely a Concert not a Conference which was desired at London, he promised to send the necessary instructions. He found many reasons, however, to postpone their dispatch and Lamb soon gave him up altogether. Esterhazy meanwhile had gone far in Palmerston's direction and was ready to establish a Concert but not a Conference at London. He tried to relieve the tension between Russia and England and urged Palmerston to make no allusion to the Treaty of Unkiar Skelessi. But this was just what Palmerston wished to do, and, as I have shown, he had warned Russia that the question of Mehemet Ali involved the question of the Straits. In November Russia gave way completely on the Persian question, too completely indeed for Austrian liking since her own services as a mediator were thus rendered less necessary. Metternich was still, however, determined that the final settlement of the Eastern Question should be negotiated under his own auspices.[2]

How much this was so was seen in the dramatic events of 1839! For when the crisis came in the spring of that year and it became clear that the Sultan was about to attack his vassal, Metternich with a sudden burst of energy took instant steps to obtain control over the negotiations. With great skill he used France as his intermediary, and,

---

[1] Palmerston to Pozzo di Borgo, 3 Sept. 1838; Nesselrode to Pozzo di Borgo, 3 Sept. 1838, *F.O. Russia*, 247; Palmerston to Clanricarde, 10 Oct. 1838, *F.O. Russia*, 243; Esterhazy to Metternich, 10 Sept. 1838, *W. St. A. England*, 285.

[2] Lamb to Palmerston, 25 Oct. 1838, *F.O. Austria*, 272; Esterhazy to Metternich, 18 Aug. (Particulière), 10 Sept. (and Particulière) 1838, *W. St. A. England*, 285.

inspired by him, the French Government proposed that a
Conference should be held at Vienna to discuss the Eastern
Question. Metternich hastened to disclaim the suggestion
of a 'Conference'. He even entreated that the word should
not be used. All he wanted, he said, was a Concert. It was
the *point d'union* to which he had so often aspired and which
at last seemed to be within his grasp.[1]

How difficult Palmerston found it to accept the invitation
is revealed by his private letters to Granville:

> We do not know what to say about a Conference at Vienna [he
> wrote on 21 June]. Metternich is so feeble and timid and tricky
> and so much swayed by Russia, and by nature so prone to crooked
> paths, to playing off one party against the other; and so fond of
> staving off difficulties and putting off the evil day, that I greatly
> doubt whether a Vienna Conference would lead to anything good.
> On the other hand Russia might perhaps consent to a Conference
> there and not elsewhere, knowing Metternich and reckoning upon
> the influence which she exerts over him and which is not the less
> real because he and Russia hate and distrust each other.[2]

But the French suggestion left Palmerston with no alter-
native unless he was to abandon the idea of a Concert
altogether. He decided, therefore, to make the best of
Metternich. 'If he could be brought to take in hand such
an arrangement as I have chalked out', he told Lamb, 'he
would do more to consolidate the peace of Europe than any
man has done since the 18th of June 1815. It would indeed
be a great settlement and why should not Austria have the
merit of settling it?' Esterhazy reported that this result was
largely due to Metternich's action at Paris.

> 'Et c'est pour cela [was Metternich's triumphant note on the
> despatch] que j'ai suivi cette nouvelle route dont le succès m'a paru
> marquant.' 'C'est donc avec d'autant plus de ménagement que
> je devais aborder ce côté délicat auprès du Principal Secrétaire
> d'Etat [confessed Esterhazy], qu'il s'agissait ni plus ni moins que

---

[1] Palmerston to Lamb, 28 June 1839, *F.O. Austria*, 278; Lamb to
Palmerston, 14 June, 15 July 1839, *F.O. Austria*, 281. Cf. *Levant Correspondence*, i. 65. Metternich, *Mémoires*, vi. 368.
[2] Palmerston to Granville, 21 June 1839, *Granville Papers*, Box 14.

de le faire renoncer à l'espoir, dont, je ne saurais en douter, il s'étoit chéri jusqu'ici, savoir celui d'exercer au moyen d'une conférence turco-égyptienne une influence bien autrement vaste sur les affaires d'Orient, à l'instar de celle qu'à l'aide de celle de Hollande-Belge ce Ministre vient incontestablement d'exercer dans les affaires de l'Ouest en Europe.'

The discussion was, however, exceedingly frank. Palmerston admitted that he was loath to allow the negotiations to go to Vienna because of Metternich's subservience to Russia, but that he had finally decided to trust him. Esterhazy was completely satisfied and claimed that he deserved a military order for 'plantant le drapeau Autrichien sur les discussions diplomatiques orientales en contribuant d'en fixer le siège à Vienne'. Metternich also was delighted and covered the dispatches with enthusiastic comments. Palmerston, he said, was like a man who had recovered at the point of death, a rare occurrence in great sinners.[1]

It was true that Britain demanded that Mehemet should be turned out of Syria altogether while France had quite a different policy. So had Metternich; but he revelled in the opportunity which the rivalry of the two Western Powers appeared to give him of re-establishing his supremacy over the negotiations, and promised support to each in turn.

Important consequences followed which more than compensated Palmerston for his self-restraint and the sacrifice of his own position. For Metternich's energy produced an apparent harmony between Governments who in reality by no means understood one another. France was drawn along and Russia was too far off to influence the situation. Her representative at Vienna followed the Austrian lead, and combined instructions were sent to Constantinople. These resulted in the Collective Note to the Sultan of 27 July, which was the basis of all future negotiations. Europe

---

[1] Palmerston to Beauvale, 20 June 1838, *Granville Papers*, Box 14; Esterhazy to Metternich, 29 June 1839 (and Particulière), *W. St. A. England*, 288; Metternich to Esterhazy, 3 July 1839, *W. St. A. England*, 291. In the quotation above Esterhazy wrote 'Est' but he clearly meant 'Ouest'.

appeared to be united in face of the catastrophe in the East. A *point d'union* had been established at Vienna. Metternich had not been so happy for years.[1]

All this time he seems to have had no doubt but that the Tsar would be only too glad to accept the lead of one who had defended him so loyally for the past nine years. The earlier rebuffs when he had in vain tried to obtain control of the Eastern Question, had had no effect upon his mind. When the Russian answer was strangely delayed he grew a little uneasy and pleaded for time, but he still declared himself confident of the result. As the delay grew out of all reason he became desperate and talked wildly of making a Quadruple Alliance without Russia.[2] At last the long-expected answer arrived from Petersburg, brought by his own Ambassador, Count Ficquelmont. It was a brutal refusal, couched in no uncertain terms and with no regard for Metternich's feelings. The Tsar had not the slightest intention of allowing Metternich to control the negotiations on the Eastern Question. He was also irritated at the report, which had reached him, that Metternich had claimed he could answer for him in any event. Perhaps, as Metternich later alleged, the fact that the proposal was pressed by the French Ambassador made him unduly suspicious. But the decision was entirely in accordance with the Tsar's previous attitude. He had never really trusted Metternich and if he was to make concessions to Britain he preferred to make them himself. He was already aware that he could not repeat the victory of 1833. He decided, therefore, to use the opportunity to drive a wedge between the two Western Powers and isolate France whose King he still hated.[3]

The blow was undoubtedly the most severe which Metter-

---

[1] Esterhazy to Metternich, 9, 24 July 1839, *W. St. A. England*, 288; Metternich to Esterhazy, 19 July 1839, *W. St. A. England*, 291.

[2] Beauvale to Palmerston, 30 July, 1, 2 Aug. 1839, *F.O. Austria*, 280, 282.

[3] Beauvale to Palmerston, 2 Sept. 1839, *F.O. Austria*, 282; Nesselrode to Meyendorff, 24 July 1839, Nesselrode, *Lettres et papiers*, vii. 287.

nich experienced before the Revolution of 1848. It incapaci-
tated him for two months from business and he completely
lost control over events. When he had recovered he found
a new situation. For the Tsar had turned to Britain, as he
had done so often before, in spite of all the violent disputes
between the two countries. At first, indeed, he had suggested that Constantinople should be made the centre of
the discussions, an idea rejected by Palmerston who assured
Esterhazy that he still desired to keep it at Vienna. Palmerston was indeed full of suspicion of Russia whom he accused
of urging on Mehemet in order to establish her own ascen-
dancy over the Porte.[1] But soon afterwards the Tsar sent
an emissary to London to open direct negotiations and,
when his first offer was rejected, returned to the attack
so that an agreement as to action was arrived at between
the two Powers. Palmerston found in Russia that support
against French protection of Mehemet Ali which he sought
in vain at Vienna, while the Tsar also agreed to Palmerston's
views upon the closing of the Straits.

Palmerston thus obtained almost without effort the object
which he had sought in 1838. There was not yet a Conference, but the *point d'union* was established at London and
Palmerston dominated the negotiations. It is no part of my
theme to-day to show the skill and courage by which in the
next eighteen months he overcame the manifold difficulties
of the problem, outmanœuvred the dissidents in his own
Cabinet, faced the threats of France, and brought all his
plans to a successful conclusion. But the story would be
incomplete without some allusion to Metternich's final
attempts to recover his position.

Palmerston had shown great consideration to Metternich when the blow fell, proposing to continue to send instructions to Vienna so that he might not feel isolated.[2] But
Metternich was forced to see a policy, the essentials of which

[1] Esterhazy to Metternich, 11, 14, 22 Aug. 1839, *W. St. A. England*,
288, 290.
[2] Bourqueney to Soult, 18 Aug. 1839, Guizot, *Mémoires*, iv. 542.

he could not but approve, carried out under other auspices than his own. The special emissary whom he sent to London was Neumann, who, I have pointed out, was no great friend of Palmerston. Nevertheless Neumann played an important part in the negotiations which enabled Palmerston at last to conclude the Treaty of 15 July 1840 and isolate France. The explosion of wrath which occurred at Paris alarmed every statesman in Europe except Palmerston himself. He remained so cheerful amid the general gloom that even his own Cabinet colleagues believed that he was insensible to the dangers of the situation, and some of his continental critics became almost frantic. Leopold of Belgium, always on the alert when there was friction between France and England, combined with Bülow in an attempt, to which Neumann gave his blessing, to remove the negotiations from Palmerston's control to Constantinople.[1] Metternich himself was hardly at first ready for such a drastic step, not yet being quite sure of the ability of any one but Palmerston to handle Russia. He had organized his own little private Conference at Königswart, where the Vienna representatives of the Great Powers, his own Ambassadors from London and Petersburg, the Papal Nuncio, and some of the official staff of the Ballplatz, spent long summer days and nights eternally discussing the Eastern Question and the repercussions which it had produced in Europe. It was inevitable that some scheme should eventually issue from this *conciliabule*. At the end of August Metternich tentatively put forward a proposal for a League between the Four Powers against France, which might perhaps develop into an organization to maintain the future peace of Europe by the renunciation of force and the creation of a permanent Conference system. Palmerston, who was occupied with organizing the means of throwing Ibrahim out of Syria, took only a minor interest in France's armaments, for he did not believe that she would use them. He had little leisure at the moment for such schemes as these. But Lord

---

[1] Beauvale to Palmerston, 31 Aug. 1840, *F.O. Austria*, 291 a.

John Russell and other members of the British Cabinet looked to Metternich to act as mediator, and Palmerston had to use the opposition of Russia to prevent them forcing his hand.[1] Metternich's embarrassment grew in the autumn; for there was great criticism at home of his own schemes for the defence of Austria and Germany. In October, now in great alarm, he proposed that a Conference should be established at some minor town, where France could meet the Four Powers, 'charged to devise means to prevent the conflict from degenerating into war in Europe'. 'He thinks', the British Ambassador explained, 'that the proposed meeting could not advantageously take place either at Paris, London, or Vienna and he recommends a place near the Rhine, the most eligible in his opinion being Wiesbaden.'[2]

Palmerston rejected this proposal without even consulting his Cabinet, to the great indignation of Lord John Russell, who was perhaps only prevented from resigning by the delicate state of the Queen's health. But Palmerston obviously thought Metternich's proposal was simply due to an attack of nerves. Events were in any case now moving so quickly that there was no time for such expedients. For by December France had ceased to threaten, Ibrahim had been driven out of Syria, and Palmerston had been triumphantly justified.

The Eastern Question, however, remained as a permanent problem, and, as soon as the main crisis was over, Metternich became once more eager to solve it. He had large but rather vague ideas. To one point, however, he always recurred. Only at Vienna could a permanent centre

[1] Beauvale to Palmerston, 29 Aug. 1840 (enclosing Memoranda by Beauvale and Ficquelmont), *F.O. Austria*, 291 a; Palmerston to Beauvale, 9 Sept., 23 Oct. 1840, *F.O. Austria*, 289; Memorandum by Lord John Russell, 18 Sept. 1840, G. P. Gooch, *Later Correspondence of Lord John Russell*, i. 15.

[2] Beauvale to Palmerston, 8 Oct. 1840 (enclosing Memorandum), *F.O. Austria*, 291 b; Palmerston to Beauvale, 23 Oct. 1840, *F.O. Austria*, 289; Spencer Walpole, *Life of Lord John Russell*, i. 359; Lloyd C. Sanders, *Lord Melbourne's Papers*, 491; Greville, *Memoirs*, iv. 355.

be established to watch over the peace of Europe and especially that of the Ottoman Empire. Geography alone established that claim, he told Esterhazy. A guarantee of the Sultan's dominions such as Palmerston had often suggested was an absurdity. What then was to be done? The Alliance of the three Eastern Powers, he confessed, was at an end. The Four Power Treaty applied only to a temporary situation. France and England were clearly no longer friends. New alignments were necessary and new machinery to express them. This statement of principle was followed a little later by a circular dispatch which dealt with the permanent preservation of peace in the East. The main thing necessary was uniformity in the advice tendered to the Sultan by the five Powers. How this was to be attained was considered with even more vagueness than usual but the British Ambassador had no hesitation in interpreting Metternich's desires:

The Prince's real objects [he explained] do not rest on the face of this despatch. He does not dare bring them openly forward but puts this forth as a feeler to try if they can be approached. They are two. The first is to obtain a renewal of the engagement taken by England, France, Austria, and Prussia in no case to accept any aggrandizement at the expense of the Turkish Empire and to complete these acts by the accession of Russia to them. The second is to establish at Vienna a central point from which instructions should be sent in common to the Ambassadors of the five Powers at Constantinople so as to ensure the uniformity of their language and conduct.[1]

Such a proposal showed how impossible it was for the ageing Metternich to learn even from the experiences of the last two years. Palmerston put the truth bluntly in an official reply. The self-denying ordinance, he said, was unwise because Russia would not assent to it. A five Power guarantee, though not so absurd as Metternich thought it, was no longer necessary to the Sultan and might tend to make him neglect his own defence.

[1] Beauvale to Palmerston, 17, 22 April, 19 May 1841, *F. O. Austria*, 298, 299.

With regard to Prince Metternich's second proposal [he continued]
that a central point of concert should be established at Vienna from
whence instructions should from time to time be sent to the representatives of the five Powers at Constantinople, that proposal is
one which Her Majesty's Government would not be much disposed to agree to. For the course pursued during the last two years
by Austria in regard to the Turco-Egyptian question has not on
the whole been so steady and consistent, nor marked with such
firmness and energy as to inspire Her Majesty's Government with
that degree of confidence in the policy of the Austrian Cabinet,
which an acquiescence in such a scheme would imply; and in fact
when the temporary engagements of the Treaty of July shall have
been fully worked out and fulfilled, perhaps the best thing will be
that the five Powers and Turkey should fall back into their usual
state of reciprocal relations.

Concert between Powers and centres of negotiations are useful
and necessary when some Treaty is in operation which not only
requires, but at the same time regulates, their common action;
but it would be very difficult to establish a permanent concert
unaccompanied by any recorded and specifick engagement.[1]

This last judgement was possibly more that of the British
Cabinet, nearly always less ready than its Foreign Minister
for continental connexions, than inspired by Palmerston
himself. But now Palmerston had obtained his immediate
objects in the Eastern Question—and indeed, in the West as
well. There was thus no pressing need for a *point d'union*,
and in resisting Metternich's wishes he expressed himself in
general terms.

Metternich was much disappointed. He broke forth once
more into abuse of Palmerston who, he told the Russian
chargé d'affaires, was impressionable, audacious, and un-
scrupulous, qualities he asserted more suitable to a lawyer
than a statesman.[2] All this was said in a vain endeavour to
disrupt the Anglo-Russian entente which had so strangely
grown out of the Eastern Question. But the Tsar had also
got what he wanted and Metternich's words had by now no
effect on his mind. He had already proposed to Palmerston

[1] Palmerston to Beauvale, 10 May, 2 June 1841, *F.O. Austria*, 297.
[2] F. Martens, *Recueil des Traités*, iv, part i. 497–8.

to make permanent the Quadruple Alliance which had been recently established on the Eastern Question. Though the British Government had rejected this proposition, as it had that of Metternich, the Tsar continued to entertain the friendliest feelings towards them. Austria on the other hand, he told the British Ambassador, could not be depended upon because of the 'timidity and vacillation' of Metternich, who 'had not the spirit of a Gentleman' and imagined that he could 'advise upon every subject' and from his closet 'direct and instruct all the world'.[1]

Metternich was in fact much farther away in 1841 than in 1830 from the realization of his wish to establish a permanent centre of European diplomacy at Vienna. His own egotism, falsity, and weakness and the conditions of his country and government made his dream an impossible one. In diagnosis Metternich was without an equal in Europe. But no one would trust him to prescribe a remedy.

[1] F. S. Rodkey, 'Anglo-Russian Negotiations about a "Permanent" Quadruple Alliance 1840–1,' *American Historical Review*, Jan. 1921, 343–9.